DON'T LET THE OLD MAN IN!

DON'T LET THE OLD MAN IN!

"You alone hold the key"

ROBERT C. GOULD

Copyright © 2016 by Robert C. Gould.

Library of Congress Control Number:		2016919108
ISBN:	Hardcover	978-1-5245-1955-1
	Softcover	978-1-5245-1954-4
	eBook	978-1-5245-1953-7

All rights reserved. No part of this book may be reproduced or transmitted in any form or by any means, electronic or mechanical, including photocopying, recording, or by any information storage and retrieval system, without permission in writing from the copyright owner.

Any people depicted in stock imagery provided by Thinkstock are models, and such images are being used for illustrative purposes only.
Certain stock imagery © Thinkstock.

Print information available on the last page.

Rev. date: 11/28/2016

To order additional copies of this book, contact:
Xlibris
1-800-455-039
www.Xlibris.com.au
Orders@Xlibris.com.au
740642

Contents

Foreword xi

Chapter 1:   As Time Flies By 1
Chapter 2:   It Began Like This for Me 3
Chapter 3:   Some Key Words to Drive Change 5
Chapter 4:   Here's How You Work 8
Chapter 5:   So What Is a Personal Affirmation
             Statement? 10
Chapter 6:   The Workshop Manual and the
             Fifteen Commandments 11
Chapter 7:   W. Shakespeare's Perspective on the
             Stages of Life 72
Chapter 8:   Dying Is Compulsory (But Leave It a While) 74

Appendix I: The Fifteen Commandments
             Daily Check Chart 77
Appendix II: The Fifteen Commandments
             Quick Reference Summary 81

To my dear wife, Kate, and our two children, Max and Anna. Thank you so much for letting me know the old man was sliding in!

Thanks too, to all those many friends and mentors who shared their thoughts with me on this manual. In particular, Mike Rigoll whose lively and energetic cartoon characters bring life to each commandment.

Author's Warning

If you believe you will live forever; if you believe you are too old to change, then read no further. Either you know it all or are just too lazy to reach for the possible. There is nothing for you here.

Foreword

Delivering a serious personal message to someone close, face to face, is a high-risk tactic. The messenger is often seriously wounded or the relationship sacrificed in the process.

This little manual evolved because I needed to deliver a message to a friend. It appeared to me (and others) that some aspects of our friend's lifestyle were unsustainable in the longer run. It concerned us deeply that our friend would "leave the party" early.

Forgive me for guessing, but it may be that a relative or close friend has given you this manual. Perhaps they feel the manual contains a message for you. They (like me) may have reasoned sensibly that they have neither the words nor the courage to deliver the message in person.

So as you turn the manual's pages you may well find yourself in nodding acknowledgement that indeed there are aspects of your lifestyle where the old man is sliding in unseen and uninvited. Without a single word being said by anyone, you will know the changes to make.

CHAPTER 1

As Time Flies By

As a man celebrates his sixtieth birthday, the seventh decade beckons. Unknowingly for many, it seems, this day is the start of the last quarter of their lifetime. It is where old age begins and the old man lurks.

For some, as with the other stages of their lives, there may be some effort needed to deal with the challenges their new circumstance brings. The term used often for such circumstance is a "crisis". So life after sixty might be coined "the last-quarter crisis".

I make no apology for what some might feel is the blunt presentation style of this little manual. It is meant to be blunt. The format is configured to prod readers; it is intended to goad them to question and to confront their current attitudes, behaviour, and approaches to their daily lives and activities as they become willing or unwilling hostages to the creeping constraints of the ageing process.

Reading this manual may well create a sense of discomfort, unease, or even worry about the current direction your life is taking in this last quarter of an average lifetime. So the reader is encouraged to take time to figure out the way forward and devise an adjusted lifestyle to deal with the changes that the last-quarter crisis may demand.

However, in this manual you will find no reference to what you should be doing with your life, whether you should work, managing your personal relationships and so on. Everyone is different; each is an individual, and each must determine what is for him.

The creeping onset of old age can be a wasting condition. The young among us are certain you are old, and you (quite naturally) believe firmly and with no doubt that you are almost as young as you have always been. Therein lies a human arcanum, a secret of nature.

It may seem obvious to many, but few of us seek to be regarded as old people; that is, to actively think, look, behave and act as old people. Nonetheless many of us, begrudgingly or otherwise, recognise and accept the reality of the ageing process and the inevitability of the arrival of old age. We have to; it is inevitable.

However, in most of us there is an innate resistance to this ageing process. Much of this resistance is weak and manifests as just a thought bubble, such as, "I don't consider myself to be old!"

Of itself this token resistance harks of a meek acceptance that the old man is already on his way in. And you would be wise to remember that we on the outside looking on can see him there in all his awful oldness. He is well and truly on his way in!

There is much advice and discussion on ageing and its effects proffered by doctors and other experts on this and that through all manner of broadcast channels. This expertise appears then to be knowingly interpreted and rebroadcast by bands of unqualified know-alls who have read, heard, or seen all that the doctors and experts have written or said.

So now for a confession. The author of this little manual is oldish (rather than old) and has no qualifications whatsoever in any form of geriatric medical practice. He is just one of those fellows who operated various businesses during his working life and managed to make a buck. He simply and gently gave staff a clear template of *what* he sought from them and marvelled at *how* they developed strategies and behaviours to adapt to circumstance and deliver what was sought of them.

So this little manual is designed to do just that: to give you a personal code and a protocol to follow for change. It is about what to do to keep the old man out, rather than how to do it.

CHAPTER 2

It Began Like This for Me

"Happy sixtieth birthday, old man. You have fifteen summers left!"

This confronting revelation was the congratulatory welcome to my seventh decade by my younger friend "Stormin'" Norman in 2008.

"You're kidding! I shall live longer than that!" I retorted.

"You may well do, my friend, but here's the thing. If you want to climb Mt. Kilimanjaro, you had better do it soon, as I doubt they'll let you on the mountain at seventy-five!"

This happy meeting shocked me into facing both the ageing of my physical frame and the inevitability of my mortality. I acknowledge now, absolutely, that each eventuality *will be*.

Some years later, my old friend Dick and I were discussing where we would like to die and how old we would like to be. We agreed on a clear and simple target for each objective. These goals then became the reason and focus for generating what we had to do now to live for the better, for longer—and in good humour.

After much thought and meaningful conversation with many, some champions and some survivors, some men, some women, this manual gradually evolved. The manual contains fifteen commandments, each with a brief anecdotal justification and affirmation statements to assist in their execution.

And so I tried living according to these commandments. After several days, my wife said I seemed to be a different, more relaxed, and calmer individual. "Are you all right?" she asked cautiously. Quite clearly, my new attitude and approach to living had quickly made a marked difference on one so close to me.

I felt so very good. So now, it's over to you to keep the old man out!

CHAPTER 3

Some Key Words to Drive Change

- Imagination
- Happiness
- Self-Control, and
- Practice

These words go to the heart of the process of change. Without some understanding of these concepts, one's ability to effect change or adapt to circumstance is reduced.

Imagination

It seems that ageing and the passage of time can stunt our ability and sometimes our desire to imagine and to dream. Perhaps it is because so many of our dreams have been realised already, so creating new dreams and aspirations requires us to think more deeply. By contrast, we see and understand clearly younger people's imaginings and dreams and their ambition to realise their dreams.

Imagination is the crucible from which dreams and aspirations are forged. It is these dreams that fire a zest for experimentation and the gathering of experiences. So fostering and firing one's imagination is crucial to looking forwards, rather than backwards. This deep, imaginative thought is crucial for an interesting and stimulating life. It is the trigger for goal setting and, of course, the creation and attainment of the ubiquitous bucket list.

Happiness

Here are some harsh realities about happiness. Some people are happy; others are less happy or even unhappy. An individual's state of happiness knows no trite definition. For all the experts' ponderings, it is a fuzzy concept.

What is clear is that an individual's state of happiness is their state of mind and no one else's. One person cannot make another happy. Just because one person bestows a benefit on another doesn't mean that person delivers happiness. One might feed another, shower gifts on another, cuddle another, and provide all manner of emotional and physical support for another. The bestowed benefit may please or delight the beneficiary, but the beneficiary's underlying state of happiness may well remain unchanged in the long run.

Happiness is determined from within the individual, and it appears to be aligned closely with a person's ability to take responsibility for their own actions and the resulting outcomes, whether for better or worse.

Unhappiness appears closely aligned with the propensity of an individual to blame others for their situation. To blame another is to delegate the power of personal responsibility or accountability to someone else. The more frequently the blaming is repeated to a different audience, the greater the resulting unhappiness would seem.

Self-Control

Self-control in various measures is at the core of every human being. Without it, humans fail either to perform on another's instruction or to accomplish a self-determined goal and outcome. Self-control is the slow-burning resolve of an individual to deliver, that is, to transform a dream into a reality or outcome.

The counterweight to self-control is impulsiveness, which may involve a hasty, ill-considered judgement of risk. Impulsiveness is an impediment and often a diversionary pothole on the road to self-actualisation.

Why is self-control important as we age? The following fifteen commandments seek self-actualisation, which arises from the mix of self-direction and determination, tempered and guided with steely self-control. The personal affirmation statements simply strengthen one's self-control. For this manual's commandments to be effective, the older, gentle individual is encouraged to develop a robust self-control mechanism. Self-control is the oxygen that gives life to the realisation of outcomes.

Practice

The saying goes that "Practice makes perfect." Upon reflection, it is clear that if what is being practised is done incorrectly then the target of perfection will be missed. In perfection's place will be the permanence of the incorrect action. For example, a regularly practised but incorrect golf swing will become a permanently incorrect golf swing. Thus, practising a changed behaviour will make permanent the result. So remember the adage this way: "Practice makes permanent."

CHAPTER 4

Here's How You Work

This is a what-to-do book. It is not a how-to-do book.

You will work out how to do what you are asking of yourself. There are planeloads of experts and know-alls who can tell you how to do all sorts of things.

Reading the script in this manual will take some forty-five minutes. There are fifteen commandments. Why "commandments?" Men understand a commandment. Moses figured that out, and the Ten Commandments applied to all.

A commandment must be simple, concise, and reasonable. Each commandment comes with its reason, together with a selection of personal affirmation statements.

The commandments written in this manual are non prescriptive. Some commandments may apply to you, and some may not. Some you will decline. It is for you to decide which to follow and which to disregard.

Select personal affirmation statements for each commandment that you believe reflect your individual approach to fulfilling that commandment. Alternatively, you may prefer to write your own (see Chapter 5). Early each day for seven days, read your commandments and your affirmation statements.

As you progress through each day, the way you live your life will begin to change. Semi-subconsciously, you will remember, acknowledge, and fulfil your commandments. This is your protocol for change.

As you fulfil a commandment, live in and relish the moment; quote quietly to yourself one or more of your affirmation statements. This simple action reinforces your revised and modified behaviour, making it easier the next time.

Then, each evening, reread your commandments and personal affirmation statements, and relive the day's outcomes. I promise you the old man won't get in!

CHAPTER 5

So What Is a Personal Affirmation Statement?

A personal affirmation statement is a short sentence that simply affirms the outcome of an individual's action. So, if losing weight is your objective, then an affirmation statement for losing weight might be, "I feel full on small helpings." Over time, gently affirming that you feel full on small helpings becomes a truth; because you do feel full on small helpings, you eat less.

Constructing a personal affirmation statement is simple; it should have the following characteristics and be individual to you:

- Be in the singular and include the words "I," "me," "my," or "mine."
- Emphasise an action by you.
- Deliver you a benefit, a good feeling, or a result.
- Emphasise the positive.
- Avoid negatives such as "not," "no," and "but."

CHAPTER 6

The Workshop Manual and the Fifteen Commandments

The remainder of this manual is a workbook. So arm yourself with a pen and work through the commandments and personal affirmation statements that will become your code and protocol.

Following each commandment there is a blank page for your personal notes and affirmations. At the back of the manual there is a thirty-one-day check chart to track your initial progress on each selected commandment. Within a short time this manual will become a well-worn manuscript unlike many other instruction books stacked in your library.

First Commandment

Accept a Social Invitation Always

A cheery crowd lifts all spirits.

As we age, many of us become more selective about the people we like to be with and when. When in this frame of mind, it becomes easy to decline a social invitation simply because the inviting party isn't really who you think you would like to be with. Often this position is compounded because your partner seeks the company of people you are less keen on (and vice versa). But getting together with others socially often produces amazing outcomes and surprises, such as meeting fresh faces and developing new and exciting plans.

Some Personal Affirmation Statements for Accepting an Invitation

- o I look forward to meeting new people.
- o I look forward to meeting old pals.
- o I enjoy telling tall stories.
- o I enjoy listening to people's stories.
- o I am careful about bettering others' experiences.
- o I am very good at remembering other people's names
- o I greet people with enthusiasm.
- o I greet people with a compliment over dress or physique.
- o I wait until others have finished talking.
- o I avoid interrupting.
- o Listening intently is easy for me.
- o Eye contact is uplifting for me.
- o Laughing at others' jokes comes easily to me.

Your Personal Affirmation Statements and Notes

Second Commandment

Be Athletic One Hour Each Day

It's the wind beneath your wings.

Most medical evidence points firmly to the benefits of regular, gentle exercise on both the mind and body. No matter how old or infirm you may be, move in any way you can for one hour each day, regularly and without compromise.

It matters not what the exercise is. Just do something with friends or on your own. The benefits are, quite simply, priceless.

Some Personal Affirmation Statements for Being Athletic

- Exercising regularly is very easy for me.
- I enjoy exercising alone with my thoughts.
- I enjoy the camaraderie when exercising with others.
- Practising my athletic skills is easy for me.
- I love to feel my body glow after exerting myself.
- I am watchful over safety when I exercise.
- I love to walk the dog.
- I know any expense outlay for exercise gives great returns of well-being to me.
- I relish the feel of wind on my face and in my hair.
- I marvel at nature when I am exercising.
- Hearing my heart beat strongly raises my spirits.
- I seek to feel extremely well.
- Taking small physical risks invigorates me.
- I always try to stand rather than sit.

Your Personal Affirmation Statements and Notes

Third Commandment

Adopt Role Models

It's OK to follow.

Role models are fabulous creations; they are there to be studied and to be copied! A role model demonstrates what can be done and sometimes how it's done. Whether it's an activity or behaviour, the role model has taken the risk in developing and customising that activity or behaviour. Emulating a role model reduces risks and saves time, and the result is known.

There are role models for all occasions and activities. Whether you seek to improve in your chosen sport or hobby, learn how to be well groomed and dressed, or react productively to some circumstance, there's a role model.

Some Personal Affirmation Statements for Adopting Role Models

- Studying how other people do well is instructive for me.
- Watching athletic people move gives me a great example.
- The accomplishments of others set me a great example of what is possible.
- The accomplishments of others give me great ideas as to what I might do.
- I find relief in asking what another would do.
- Matching a role model's achievements is invigorating for me.
- I understand well that no one is perfect.
- Asking others how they achieved great things is easy for me.
- Watching and listening to talented musicians inspires me.

Your Personal Affirmation Statements and Notes

Fourth Commandment

Be a Gentle Man

Now is your time for gentleness.

As the testosterone ebbs away and past physical feats fade in the memory, it is time to develop the magic of gentleness. It takes strength to be gentle and to lock out the anger, bitterness, and grumpiness that are often just lonely remnants of a former indulgent "manliness." Family, friends, and others, particularly women, are drawn magically toward the firm gentleness and quiet self-confidence of the gentle man.

Some Personal Affirmation Statements for Being a Gentle Man

- I move away when I begin to feel angry.
- I avoid useless argument.
- I feel comfortable yielding graciously.
- I practise hard to be well-mannered and courteous.
- Unconditional forgiveness comes easily to me.
- Being angry is just not me.
- I actively seek to make friends with people's pets.
- I waste no time on regret.
- There is precious time left for me to rue past mistakes.
- I seek to avoid aggressiveness in any form.
- Being polite is easy for me.
- People's feelings matter to me.
- I acknowledge that what people think of me is their business.
- I make time to smell my roses deeply.
- Smiling and laughing come easily and are rewarding for me.
- I understand that being a gentle man costs nothing.
- I am always courteous in traffic.
- When dealing with aggressive nastiness I am calm, quiet, and resolute.

Your Personal Affirmation Statements and Notes

Fifth Commandment

Dress Half Your Age

Don't let the old man in.

It appears that with ageing comes a subconscious dowdiness. Just look around at a gathering of older citizens and you will undoubtedly see slumping physiques shrouded in dull, colourless, and shapeless garments that may have been of a vogue long since past.

It is so easy to keep wearing those comfortable clothes you have had for ages – but this is where the old man gets in! When you look older, others see you as older and treat you as older. So now you *are* older. The old man is well and truly in!

Change requires courage. Do it gradually. Seek counsel of someone suave. Pick a role model. Compliment others on their appearance, and you will follow in becoming well groomed.

Some Personal Affirmation Statements for Dressing Half Your Age

- I find mild eccentricity in my dress sense energising.
- I feel younger when I dress well.
- Looking elegant is what people expect of me.
- I am pleased when my family remark on my good dress sense.
- I aim to be stylish.
- Wearing colour enlivens me.
- My favourite colour is ……
- I take pride in acquiring new clothes.
- I know that my clothes fit well on my new physique.
- I enjoy wearing colour.
- I am careful about being fashionable.

Your Personal Affirmation Statements and Notes

Sixth Commandment

Watch Over Your Family

You are needed there always.

Families have some similarities with corporate structures. Both have culture and traditions, policies and procedures, rules, regulations, principles and discipline and, of course, methods of managing money and wealth (or lack thereof).

As an older man, you could view the responsibilities of watching over your family as a promotion to a non-executive role on the family's board of directors. I say your new role is non-executive because as your family members grow older, they no longer need your executive decision-making. Instead they seek your respectful interest and watchful guidance. You are a readily available source of wisdom.

This new role becomes one of fostering a family atmosphere that encourages the younger members to dream and to realise those dreams. Be careful and perhaps slow with advancing cash to family members; make sure your affairs are in order with a properly prepared and executed will. A messy estate is a breeding ground for family unrest and squabbling on a grand scale when you die.

Some Personal Affirmation Statements for Watching Over Your Family

- I am quietly proud of my children's achievements.
- Giving to family is easy for me.
- Putting my family before me is easy for me.
- I enjoy laughing with my family.
- I am slow to be critical of my family's choices.
- I love the banter of family mealtime conversations.
- I am warmed by celebrating family events well.
- Others' birthdays are important to me.
- I work hard to keep the door open for family members.
- I am glad for my family that my affairs are in order.

Your Personal Affirmation Statements and Notes

Seventh Commandment

Mow Your Own Lawn

Each good job done takes you higher.

There may be no "lawn" and no "mower," but developing self-reliance is a wonderful goal. Relying on others to do simple tasks can be tedious.

Many working lives were spent in unfulfilling, tedious, and repetitive roles which produced little by way of personal satisfaction or lasting reward compared with the more personal actions of making, building, maintaining, and repairing items about the home.

The benefits of this move to self-reliance might be order, exercise, and a spell in the fresh air. Clearly, being self-reliant gives confidence to those near and dear to you that you can look after yourself. "I did that by myself" is a very powerful personal affirmation.

Some Personal Affirmation Statements for Mowing My Lawn

- o   I get great satisfaction from doing things for myself.
- o   I am great at composing to-do lists.
- o   I enjoy ticking off the items.
- o   I like to seek advice from friends.
- o   I relish the physical exertion of activities and tasks.
- o   I leave working at heights on ladders to others.
- o   Self-reliance is important for me as an example to my family.
- o   I like to learn by helping tradesmen when they visit.
- o   I enjoy the feeling of friendship resulting from helping others with tasks or projects.
- o   I am proud when friends comment on the results of my work.

Your Personal Affirmation Statements and Notes

Eighth Commandment

Do a Good Turn Each Day

It nourishes your soul.

While this commandment has a Boy Scout feel to it, doing a good turn really is an uplifting experience. This act is served best with a generosity of spirit and kindness often ignited with that spark named spontaneity.

Of course, a good turn may involve far more than helping someone cross the road. It may be regular volunteering for a charity or any other activity or action that promotes selflessness and a desire to assist others in need.

Some Personal Affirmation Statements for Doing a Good Turn

- I am acutely conscious that I have so much and others so little.
- I seek opportunities to assist people less fortunate than me.
- I seek the inner glow that comes from a well-meant "thank you."
- Helping ease someone else's burden is easy for me.
- Making charitable donations is important for me.
- I look forward to my charitable work each week.
- Visiting patients in hospital is a pleasure for me.
- Being sympathetic towards those who are suffering is easy for me.
- I enjoy surprising people with small gifts.
- I enjoy doing random acts of kindness.

Your Personal Affirmation Statements and Notes

Ninth Commandment

Foster a Sense of the Ridiculous

Die smiling.

Having a sense of fun often arises from having a trained eye and ear attuned and alert to seeing the funny side of circumstance and realising that being too serious can be limiting. For goodness' sake, just how serious can you be, really?

Seeing the funny side avoids frivolousness and is never personal unless the object of mirth is a self-promoting, pompous fool. Family, friends, and others are attracted to those of good humour, ready smiles, bright eyes, and a lightness of being.

Some Personal Affirmation Statements for Sensing the Ridiculous

- I smile readily at the incongruous.
- I smile at the way people see life.
- I am energised by mild eccentricity.
- I am amused by others' sense of what is fun.
- Some silly things I do make me smile.
- Laughing at myself with others energises me.
- Smiling and laughing are easy for me.
- I see humour in many things.
- Seeing the funny side is easy for me.
- "Wow! Look at that!" is a favourite expression of mine.

Your Personal Affirmation Statements and Notes

Tenth Commandment

Drop the Drink

No man ever died from alcoholic abstinence.

For many men, the immediate reaction to this commandment is, "No! Not me! I love a drink, and I am not going to compromise my fun!"

But in this commandment the word "drop" is purposely ambiguous. Either you can "drop" as in stop all together and become a teetotaller or "drop" as in reduce your consumption.

It is blindingly obvious to many men as they age that their bodies will not cope with their alcoholic intake at, say, sixty when they reach eighty. This commandment raises the issue of alcohol consumption. It is for the individual to question their alcoholic intake, that is, to think again.

Some Personal Affirmation Statements for Dropping the Drink

- I like hot tea in the early evening.
- I enjoy the time I have to think without booze.
- I sip and savour a drink slowly.
- I am comfortable refusing top-ups.
- I rarely drink at lunchtime.
- I never drink before 1:00 p.m.
- I am inventive in cocktailing non-alcoholic beverages.
- I am good at sitting on one drink.
- I count accurately the beers I drink by keeping the bottle tops.
- I am proud of my self-control when I say no and mean it.
- I am an expert at putting off the first drink.
- I believe strongly that drinking wastes my time.

Your Personal Affirmation Statements and Notes

Eleventh Commandment

Lose Weight; Just Shrink

There are no fat old men.

Well, there may be a few fat old men, but chances are they will not be around for long! There seems to be little argument among the medical experts on this subject that being old and fat is a serious health hazard. And so, since becoming younger is no option, becoming slimmer and smaller is the only way.

Seriously, if you are in life for the long haul and you are overweight, then you should shrink. Fit old people tend to be lean. How you do it is up to you. There are all manner of experts on weight loss eager to help you.

Of course, there's the age-old question for each individual as to what is old and what is fat! Even if you are fit but fat, there is little guarantee that in the long run the fitness will overcome the fatness.

Consider this question. How do you handicap a racing thoroughbred? Just place weights under the saddle to slow the animal down. How much weight? The average added weight is some 3 kilos or 6.6 pounds. The average thoroughbred weighs 475 kilos or 1,000 pounds. So if you are carrying an extra three kilos on a frame of a hundred kilos or less, you are seriously handicapping yourself.

Some Personal Affirmation Statements for Shrinking and Losing Weight.

- I feel well fed on small helpings.
- I enjoy eating fresh vegetables.
- I like to feel slightly hungry.
- Snacks are bonuses I have yet to earn.
- I take my time to eat properly.
- I enjoy savouring each mouthful.
- I am shrinking my waist to half my height.
- I regard sardines as a miracle food.
- I always leave something on my plate.
- I anticipate declining a second helping.
- I always decline second helpings politely.
- I regard (insert food) as toxic and poisonous to my good health.
- Losing weight is easy for me.
- I like to stand rather than sit.
- My favourite saying is "I couldn't eat another thing."

Your Personal Affirmation Statements and Notes

Twelfth Commandment

(S)train Your Brain

Or lose your mind.

Like weight management, there's much said about this topic by all manner of experts and know-alls. The reality seems to be that engagement in any form of mental stimulation is beneficial. So it seems it is a matter of each to his own, be it music, intellectual discussion, cards, jokes, reading, or crosswords.

Brains are like brawn. Some have wonderfully agile brains and others the reverse. Nonetheless, lively conversation and social activity appear to be excellent for provoking mental stimulation.

Some Personal Affirmation Statements for (S)training Your Brain

- I relish the challenge of learning new things.
- I like to complete a crossword every day.
- Learning new technologies stimulates me.
- I am proud when people comment on my technical skills.
- I rise to the challenge of word games.
- I enjoy the challenge of card games.
- Composing and painting pictures absorbs me.
- Art and craft design challenge my creativity.
- I look forward to the camaraderie of card games.
- Using my imagination to do things differently invigorates me.
- I relish discussion on unfamiliar topics.
- I am invigorated by others' challenges to my reasoning.
- Sitting in silence relaxes me.
- Sitting in silence allows me to think with clarity.
- I limit my use of TV and radio.
- Singing concentrates my senses.
- Being artistic excites me.

Your Personal Affirmation Statements and Notes

Thirteenth Commandment

Live Within Your Means

Money is not important, but it's up there with oxygen.

Many will outlive their retirement savings. So it is important to develop financial toughness, to deal with the financial facts of one's position, and to avoid fighting them. To develop this financial toughness a mix of practices is needed, including paying for sound financial advice, testing expenditure ruthlessly, being wary of credit, minimising tax and maximising welfare, and emulating others of similar standing who appear to be managing their money well.

Some Personal Affirmation Statements for Living Within Your Means

- Realistic budgeting is easy for me.
- It easy for me to defer discretionary expenditure.
- I do well at making do.
- I am very comfortable driving a small car.
- I enjoy riding on public transport.
- I am good at saying, "I can go without that."
- I stay well away from the Joneses.
- I am uninterested in other people's money or lack of it.
- I avoid comparing my wealth with others.
- I readily acknowledge that I am fortunate.
- Owing money makes me uncomfortable.
- Paying bills early is good for my well-being.
- I take comfort that my affairs are in order.

Your Personal Affirmation Statements and Notes

Fourteenth Commandment

Unload Stuff; Let It Go

Travel light; travel far.

In the early years many embark on an accumulation phase. There is competition for the best cars, houses, boats, and other stuff that promises to make our lives better and to distinguish competitors from each other. In the middle years this accumulation period morphs into a holding, make-do-with, or simple replacement phase.

As age wearies the material man struggling with maintaining this menagerie of stuff, the last phase begins: that is, to unload and declutter. This last phase appears to be the easiest, but in reality many of these former objects of desire hold sweet memories or fall into the "I might need that" trap. The question to be asked is, "Does it add to my state of happiness?" In the end junk is junk, and you really can't take it with you!

Try this. Pack an aircraft carry-on bag and live from it for a week. You will be amazed how little you miss everything else!

Some Personal Affirmation Statements for Unloading Your Stuff

- Throwing stuff away is easy for me.
- I feel free when I give stuff away.
- I enjoy the freedom from ownership obligation.
- I enjoy seeing people use stuff I no longer use.
- I enjoy seeing people value stuff I no longer value.
- Storing stuff is a burden on me.
- I look forward to and diarise any government junk collections.
- I love to travel with a carry-on bag only.

Your Personal Affirmation Statements and Notes

Fifteenth Commandment

Aspire to a Simple Life

It's more complex than it appears.

There is no such business as a simple one, and no one lives a simple life. Without disciplined thought, an uncomplicated action or idea invariably develops its own unforeseen web of complexity. These webs of complexity feed on each other, eating into time, and often develop into confoundedness for an ageing individual.

Now is the time to get out of this and get out of that. Cut back on and disengage from activities and pursuits that create more hassle and mental anguish than they return in well-being. Be wary of compounding your own life's complexities with those of others.

Some Personal Affirmation Statements for Aspiring to a Simple Life

- I enjoy the time I have, free of worry.
- Keeping my affairs in order is easy for me.
- I avoid discussions on subjects over which I have no influence.
- I am good at being neat and tidy.
- I work hard to clear messiness.
- Messiness complicates life for me.
- I enjoy the feeling of creating order from chaos.
- I aspire to normal blood pressure readings.

Your Personal Affirmation Statements and Notes

CHAPTER 7

W. Shakespeare's Perspective on the Stages of Life

In his play *As You Like It*, William Shakespeare compares the world to a stage and life to a play. The play's actors are the seven stages of a man's life. These seven stages include the infant, schoolboy, lover, soldier, justice, pantaloon, and old age or second childishness.

This manual's interest lies in the last three stages described thus:

"And then, the Justice
In fair round belly, with a good capon lined,
With eyes severe, and beard of formal cut,
Full of wise saws, and modern instances,
And so he plays his part.
The sixth age shifts into the lean and slippered pantaloon,
with spectacles on nose and pouch on side,
His youthful hose, well saved, a world too wide for his shrunk shank, and
His big manly voice, turning again toward childish treble, pipes and whistles in his sound.
Last scene of all, that ends this strange eventful history,
Is second childishness and mere oblivion,
Sans teeth, sans eyes, sans taste, sans everything."

For Shakespeare it appears that our old man is gently signalling his menacing presence in the justice with his "fair round belly." And then our old man brazenly takes up residence in the stooping pantaloon (funny old man) with his slippers and oversized, baggy trousers. Sadly, he seems to have neglected the fifth commandment, as he is still wearing his old "hose" and thus failing to dress half his age. The good news is his obedience to the eleventh commandment, evidenced by his "shrunk shank!"

Four hundred years ago Shakespeare died at home on his birthday in 1616 after a lengthy birthday party drinking with companions at a local hostelry. Arguably, at fifty-two years old, he was too young to be a subject for the commandments in this manual. Nonetheless, he failed to obey the manual's tenth commandment to "drop the drink." However, he had obeyed the first commandment to "accept a social invitation, always!"

Perhaps one day, you and I shall meet after accepting a social invitation. I look forward to that day.

CHAPTER 8

Dying Is Compulsory (But Leave It a While)

"Look at you, Susie! When's that baby due?"

"The doctor told me it'll be March 26. I am so excited!"

"Wow! How wonderful. I'm sure everything will be just fine. We'll be thinking of you."

If ever there was a target, a bullseye in life, it is a birthday. Mother-to-be Susie's life will now gravitate toward that day. Consciously and subconsciously her mind and her body will be readying for the safe delivery of her baby and homecoming on or about March 26.

However, there is no such date stamp at the other end of our lifecycle! No one has ever asked me what age I plan to be when I die. Most people, including doctors, assume that each of us will want to live just as long as we possibly can. But how long is that, exactly? "As long as possible" is a wishy-washy hope. It is no target; it is nothing to aim at.

Earlier in the manual, I mentioned that my old friend Dick and I had discussed how long we would like to live and when and where we would like to die. After a lengthy discussion on topics such as our health, family history, and respective gene pools, I chose the age of ninety to be my final year. For me it seemed attainable. It was a nice, round number—and fifteen summers more than Stormin' Norman had given me on my sixtieth birthday! The challenge of meeting a well-set, meaningful personal goal is one of life's great motivations.

Like Susie, but at the age of sixty-eight, I am now aiming at a clear target with a bullseye of ninety. It is a death wish with a difference!

That discussion with Dick was the genesis of this manual. The commandments have become my motivational code for a better, longer, and more good-humoured life. Following my code now, I am adjusting my lifestyle gently (consciously and subconsciously) to focus on *living* to the age of ninety. I can sense that obeying the commandments and repeating my personal affirmation statements is steering me toward that goal.

But that is enough from me about me. I have no more to add. So, now is the moment to wish you well on a similar journey to your chosen date with destiny, emboldened with your whispered war cry: *"Don't Let the Old Man In!"*

---The End---

The Fifteen Commandments Daily Check Chart

After considering and selecting the commandments to obey, chart your progress for your first thirty-one days by checking the boxes below.

1. Accept a social invitation always.

1	2	3	4	5	6	7	8	9	10	11	12	13	14	15	
16	17	18	19	20	21	22	23	24	25	26	27	28	29	30	31

2. Be athletic one hour each day.

1	2	3	4	5	6	7	8	9	10	11	12	13	14	15	
16	17	18	19	20	21	22	23	24	25	26	27	28	29	30	31

3. Adopt role models.

1	2	3	4	5	6	7	8	9	10	11	12	13	14	15	
16	17	18	19	20	21	22	23	24	25	26	27	28	29	30	31

4. Be a gentle man.

1	2	3	4	5	6	7	8	9	10	11	12	13	14	15	
16	17	18	19	20	21	22	23	24	25	26	27	28	29	30	31

5. Dress half your age.

1	2	3	4	5	6	7	8	9	10	11	12	13	14	15	
16	17	18	19	20	21	22	23	24	25	26	27	28	29	30	31

6. Watch over family.

1	2	3	4	5	6	7	8	9	10	11	12	13	14	15	
16	17	18	19	20	21	22	23	24	25	26	27	28	29	30	31

7. Mow your own lawn.

1	2	3	4	5	6	7	8	9	10	11	12	13	14	15	
16	17	18	19	20	21	22	23	24	25	26	27	28	29	30	31

8. Do a good turn each day.

1	2	3	4	5	6	7	8	9	10	11	12	13	14	15	
16	17	18	19	20	21	22	23	24	25	26	27	28	29	30	31

9. Foster a sense of the ridiculous.

1	2	3	4	5	6	7	8	9	10	11	12	13	14	15	
16	17	18	19	20	21	22	23	24	25	26	27	28	29	30	31

10. Drop the drink.

1	2	3	4	5	6	7	8	9	10	11	12	13	14	15	
16	17	18	19	20	21	22	23	24	25	26	27	28	29	30	31

11. Lose weight; just shrink.

1	2	3	4	5	6	7	8	9	10	11	12	13	14	15	
16	17	18	19	20	21	22	23	24	25	26	27	28	29	30	31

12. (S)train your brain.

1	2	3	4	5	6	7	8	9	10	11	12	13	14	15	
16	17	18	19	20	21	22	23	24	25	26	27	28	29	30	31

13. Live within your means.

1	2	3	4	5	6	7	8	9	10	11	12	13	14	15	
16	17	18	19	20	21	22	23	24	25	26	27	28	29	30	31

14. Unload stuff; let it go.

1	2	3	4	5	6	7	8	9	10	11	12	13	14	15	
16	17	18	19	20	21	22	23	24	25	26	27	28	29	30	31

15. Aspire to a simple life.

1	2	3	4	5	6	7	8	9	10	11	12	13	14	15	
16	17	18	19	20	21	22	23	24	25	26	27	28	29	30	31

The Fifteen Commandments Quick Reference Summary

1. Accept a social invitation always.
2. Be athletic one hour each day.
3. Adopt role models.
4. Be a gentle man.
5. Dress half your age.
6. Watch over family.
7. Mow your own lawn.
8. Do a good turn each day.
9. Foster a sense of the ridiculous.
10. Drop the drink.
11. Lose weight; just shrink.
12. (S)train your brain.
13. Live within your means.
14. Unload stuff; let it go.
15. Aspire to a simple life.

Made in the USA
San Bernardino, CA
04 March 2019